To Hermione
For being good.
MERRY CHRISTMAS!
From Santa

Santa is coming to
Kent

Written by Steve Smallman
Illustrated by Robert Dunn and Jeremy Pyke
Designed by Sarah Allen

First published by HOMETOWN WORLD in 2013
Hometown World Ltd
7 Northumberland Buildings
Bath BA1 2JB

www.hometownworld.co.uk

ISBN 978-1-84993-397-1

Printed in China
HTW_PO220716

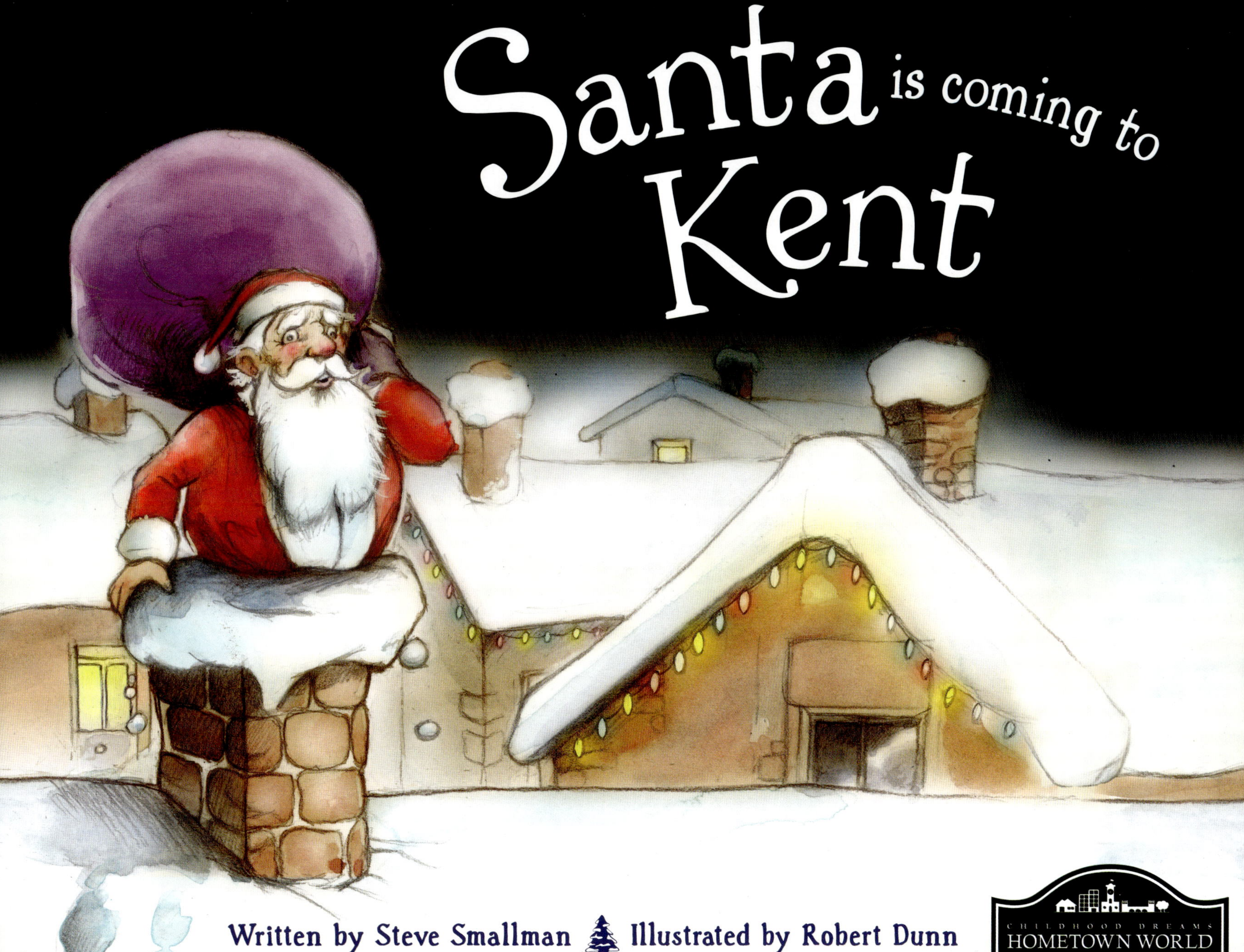
Santa is coming to
Kent
Written by Steve Smallman
Illustrated by Robert Dunn
CHILDHOOD DREAMS
HOMETOWN WORLD

boomed Santa. "Have all the children from **Kent** been good this year?"

"Well...erm...mostly," answered the little old elf, as he bustled across the busy workshop to Santa's desk.

Santa peered down at the elf from behind the tall, teetering piles of letters that the children of Kent had sent him.

"Mostly?" asked Santa, looking over the top of his glasses.

"Yes...but they've all been **especially** good in the last few days!" said the elf.

"Jolly good!" chuckled Santa.
"Then we'd better get their presents loaded up!"

Even though the sack of presents was

really, really big

and the elves were really, really small,

they seemed to have no trouble loading it onto Santa's sleigh. Though how they managed to fit such a big sack onto one little sleigh even they didn't know. But somehow they did.

"Splendid!" boomed Santa. "We're ready to go!"

"Er...not quite, Santa," said the little old elf. "One of our reindeer is missing!"

"Missing?

Which reindeer is missing?" asked Santa.

"The youngest one, Santa," said the elf. "It's his first flight tonight. I've called him and called him, but..."

Just then, a young reindeer strolled up, munching on a large carrot.

"Where have you been?"

asked Santa.

The youngest reindeer was crunching so loudly that it was no wonder he hadn't heard the little old elf calling.

"Oh well, never mind," said Santa, giving the reindeer a little wink. He took out his Santa-nav and tapped in the postcode for Kent.

"This will guide us to Kent in no time."

With a flick of the reins and a jerk of the harness, off they went, racing through the sky.

"Ho-ho-ho!"

laughed Santa.

"We'll soon have these parcels delivered to the Garden of England!"

Santa's sleigh flew through the starry night heading south across the North Sea. On they flew in the crisp, wintry air over Whitstable. In the wink of an eye, the sleigh was flying above Faversham and on over the Kent Downs. The youngest reindeer was very excited. He had never been away from the North Pole before.

They were just crossing over the Pilgrims Way
when, suddenly, they ran into a blizzard.
Snowflakes whirled around the sleigh.

They couldn't see a thing!

The youngest reindeer was getting a bit worried,
but Santa didn't seem concerned.

"In two kilometres..."

said the Santa-nav in a bossy lady's voice,

"...keep left at the next star."

"But, Madam," Santa blustered, "I can't see any stars in all this snow!"
Soon they were

hopelessly lost!

Then, through the howling blizzard, the youngest reindeer heard a faint ringing sound.

He looked over at the old reindeer with the red nose. But he had his head down.

Ding-dong! Ding-dong!

There was that sound again, like church bells ringing. The youngest reindeer turned round to look at Santa. But Santa wasn't listening. He seemed to be arguing with a little box with buttons on it.

With a flick of the harness and a jerk of the reins, the youngest reindeer gave a sharp **tug** and headed off towards the sound of the bells, pulling Santa and his sleigh behind him!

"Whoa!"

cried Santa, pulling his hat straight. "What's going on?" Then, to his surprise, he heard a ringing sound.

"Well done, young reindeer!" he shouted cheerfully. "It must be the bells of All Saints in Maidstone. Don't worry, children, Santa is coming!"

But, suddenly...

CRUNCH!

The sleigh hit something as it plummeted through the snow clouds.
"You have arrived!"
said the Santa-nav unhelpfully.

Finally, when the snow had died down and the clouds parted, Santa discovered exactly where they were...

...stuck, right at the very top of the Christmas tree outside **Maidstone Town Hall!**

"Everybody, **PULL!**"

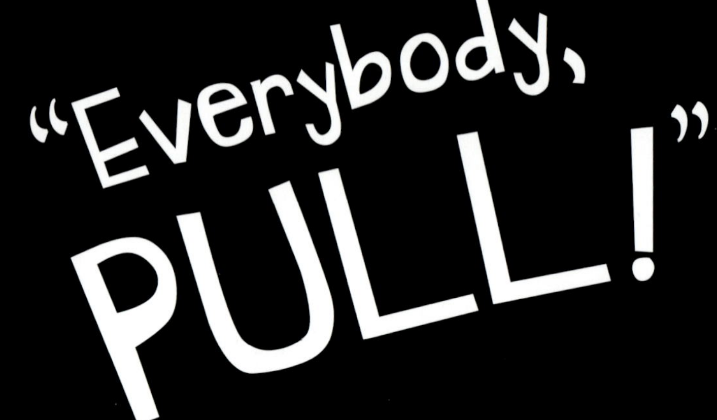

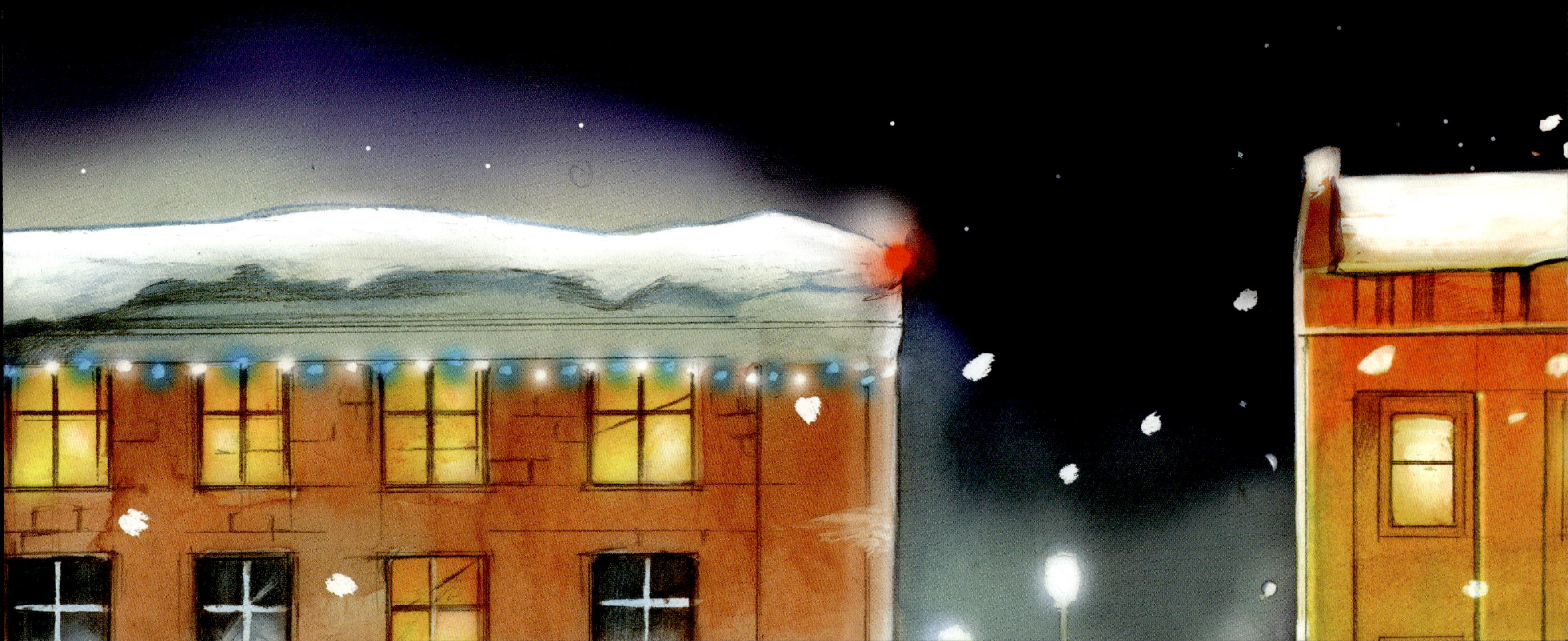

The reindeer *pulled* with all their might until, at last, with a screeching noise, the sleigh scraped clear of the Christmas tree and Santa steered them safely over Maidstone Museum, above the railway bridge, across the River Medway and down into Whatman Park.

Luckily, there was no real damage done, but the parcels had all been jumbled up. Santa quickly sorted the presents into order again.

"Right," said Santa. "Thanks to this young reindeer I know where we are now. Don't worry, children,

Santa is coming!"

Santa drove his sleigh expertly from rooftop to rooftop all over Kent, popping in and out of chimneys as fast as he could go.

(Which was pretty fast for a chubby chap!)

There were big chimneys in Royal Tunbridge Wells and small chimneys in Sandwich. He squeezed down thin chimneys in Sittingbourne and plummeted down fat chimneys in Canterbury.

The youngest reindeer was amazed at how quickly they went. Santa never seemed to get tired at all! And it looked like the children in Kent were going to be very lucky this year! But the youngest reindeer was starting to feel a bit weary and quite hungry too.

In house after house, Santa delved inside his sack for parcels of every shape and size.

He piled them under the Christmas trees and carefully filled up the stockings with surprises.

In house after house, the good children of Kent had left out a large mince pie, a small glass of something and a big, crunchy carrot.

Santa took a little bite out of each mince pie, a tiny sip of something, wiped his beard and popped the carrots into his sack.

From Dartford to Dover, from Folkestone to Faversham, from Margate to Sevenoaks and ALL the places in between, Santa and his sleigh visited every house in Kent.

Santa delivered presents to Aiden, Ava, Ben, Brooke, Cameron, Chloe...the list went on and on! ...Zak, Zara, Zybil.

Finally, Santa had delivered the last present on his long Kent list.

"Great moons and stars!" sighed Santa. "It's past midnight and my sack seems as heavy as ever! I hope I haven't forgotten anyone."

Santa opened his sack to check...but it was full of juicy, crunchy carrots!

Santa shared out the carrots between all the reindeer.
"Well done, lad!" he said, patting the youngest reindeer gently on the nose.

But the youngest reindeer didn't hear him...he was too busy munching!

Then it was time to set off for home. Santa reset his Santa-nav for the North Pole and soon they were speeding across the Swale, over the Isle of Sheppey through the crisp, starry night.

"Ho-ho-ho!"
laughed Santa.
"Merry Christmas,
Kent!"